10/04

10/09

Cockroaches Up Close

Robin Birch

Raintree

Chicago, Illinois

© 2005 Raintree

Published by Raintree, a division of Reed Elsevier, Inc.

Chicago, Illinois

Customer Service 888-363-4266

Visit our website at www.raintreelibrary.com

For information, address the publisher:
Raintree, 100 N. LaSalle, Suite 1200, Chicago, IL 60602

09 08 07 06 05
10 9 8 7 6 5 4 3 2 1

Printed and bound in Hong Kong and China by WKT Company Limited.

Library of Congress Cataloging-in-Publication Data
Birch, Robin.
   Cockroaches up close / Robin Birch.
      p. cm. -- (Minibeasts up close)
   Includes bibliographical references (p. 30).
   ISBN 1-4109-1139-X -- ISBN 1-4109-1146-2
   1. Cockroaches--Juvenile literature. I. Title. II. Series:
Birch, Robin. Minibeasts up close.
   QL505.5.B57 2004
   595.7'28--dc22
                              2004003110

Acknowledgments
The publisher would like to thank the following for permission to reproduce photographs:
p. 4 Gusto/Science Photo Library; pp. 5, 14, 15, 21, 24, 26, 27 Jiri Lochman/Lochman Transparencies; p. 6 Paul Zborowski; p. 7 David Knowles/Lochman Transparencies ; p. 8 David Scharf/ Science Photo Library ; p. 10 Heather Angel/Natural Visions; p. 11 National Geographic; pp. 12, 20, 25 Kathie Atkinson/ Auscape; p. 13 Jim Zuckerman/ APL/Corbis; p. 16 Jeff Wright/ Queensland Museum; p. 17 Stone/Getty Images; p. 19 Australian Museum; p. 28 Adrian Davis/Bruce Coleman Inc.; p. 29 AAP.

Cover photograph of a cockroach reproduced with permission of Jeff Wright/Queensland Museum.

Every effort has been made to contact copyright holders of any material reproduced in this book. Any omissions will be rectified in subsequent printings if notice is given to the publisher.

Contents

Amazing Cockroaches! 4

Where Do Cockroaches Live? 6

Cockroach Body Parts 8

Mouthparts and Eating 10

Eyes and Seeing 12

Antennae and Sensing 14

Legs for Moving 16

Wings and Flying 18

The Thorax and Abdomen 20

Inside a Cockroach 22

Cockroach Eggs 24

Young Cockroaches 26

Cockroaches and Us 28

Find Out for Yourself 30

Glossary 31

Index 32

Any words appearing in bold, **like this,** are explained in the Glossary.

Amazing Cockroaches!

Have you seen a cockroach? Was that cockroach running so fast you could not see what it was?

Cockroaches are amazing when you get to know them close up. They will eat almost anything! They are sometimes pests in houses because they get into food and leave a smelly mess behind.

Some cockroaches enter houses to look for food.

What are cockroaches?

Cockroaches are insects. An insect has six legs. It also has a hard skin on the outside of its body called an **exoskeleton,** instead of bones inside its body.

There are nearly 4,000 kinds, or **species,** of cockroaches in the world. The smallest is about as long as a large sesame seed. The largest is about as long as a computer mouse.

Cockroaches are beetle-like insects.

Where Do Cockroaches Live?

Most **species** of cockroaches live in warm, moist places.

Cockroaches often live in forests, where they can find food easily. Some cockroaches live in caves, holes in rocks, and in hollow trees. They find food that has fallen into their homes. Some live in rotting wood, and eat it. Other cockroaches live some of the time in water. They can swim and dive.

Cockroaches are flat insects, which makes it easy for them to squeeze through narrow spaces.

How do they live?

Most cockroaches are **nocturnal** and hide during the day. They find a small space to rest in, such as under stones, logs, or bark. They search for food and water at night. Most cockroaches stay near the ground.

Some cockroaches live in dry deserts. At night they stick their tongues out to collect moisture from the air.

Some kinds of cockroaches run in the treetops during the day.

Tiny cockroaches

Attaphila fungicola cockroaches are about as long as a large sesame seed. They live underground in ant nests. They ride on the backs of ants in the nest and on ants flying through the forest.

A cockroach body has three parts. These are the head, the **thorax** in the middle, and the **abdomen** at the end.

The head

The head has eyes, mouthparts, and feelers called **antennae** on it. The head bends downward.

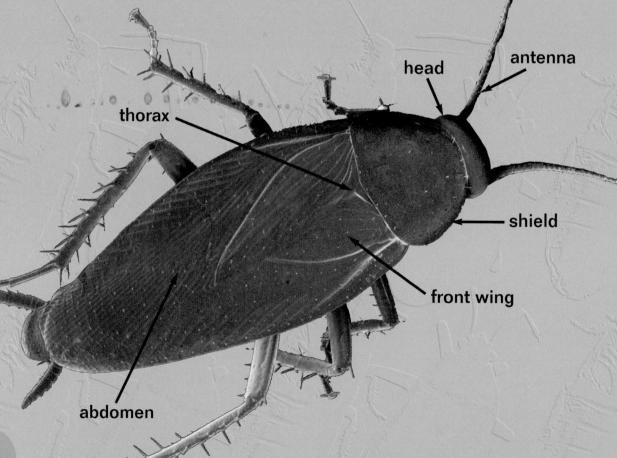

head

antenna

thorax

shield

front wing

abdomen

The thorax

The thorax has six legs on it. Most cockroaches have four wings attached to the thorax as well. The cockroach has a **shield** on the back of its thorax.

The abdomen

A cockroach's abdomen is usually covered by its wings, so you cannot see it.

The exoskeleton

The **exoskeleton** covers a cockroach's whole body, even its eyes. It is about as thick as a person's hair. The exoskeleton makes the cockroach's shape. It protects the cockroach from being hurt and keeps it from drying out by trapping water inside its body. There are hairs and **spines** on the exoskeleton.

Mouthparts and Eating

Cockroaches eat almost any kind of food. They eat leaves and fruit on trees. In forests, they clean up the forest floor by eating dead and rotting plants and animals. They are good hunters, and can catch insects such as termites, flies, wasps, and mosquitoes.

In houses, they like sweet things, such as bread and cookies. Cockroaches may also eat old books and wallpaper.

Cockroaches eat almost anything, including books!

Jaws

Cockroaches have two large, strong **jaws,** one on each side of the mouth. The jaws open and close sideways, and they have strong teeth on the ends.

Cockroaches have two smaller jaws inside the others. They clean their **antennae** and legs with these jaws.

Cockroach cannibals

Some cockroaches eat other cockroaches. The young of the German cockroach sometimes eat each other if they are too crowded together.

Palps

Cockroaches have four small **palps,** like fingers, under their mouths, two on each side. Cockroaches feel and taste their food with the palps before they eat it.

Cockroaches use their palps to feel and taste food.

Eyes and Seeing

A cockroach has two large eyes. Each eye is made up of 2,000 very small eyes. This kind of eye is called a **compound** eye. The small eyes are all packed closely together. Each small eye faces in a slightly different direction, and sees something a little bit different from the other small eyes.

All cockroaches have two large eyes, one on each side of the head.

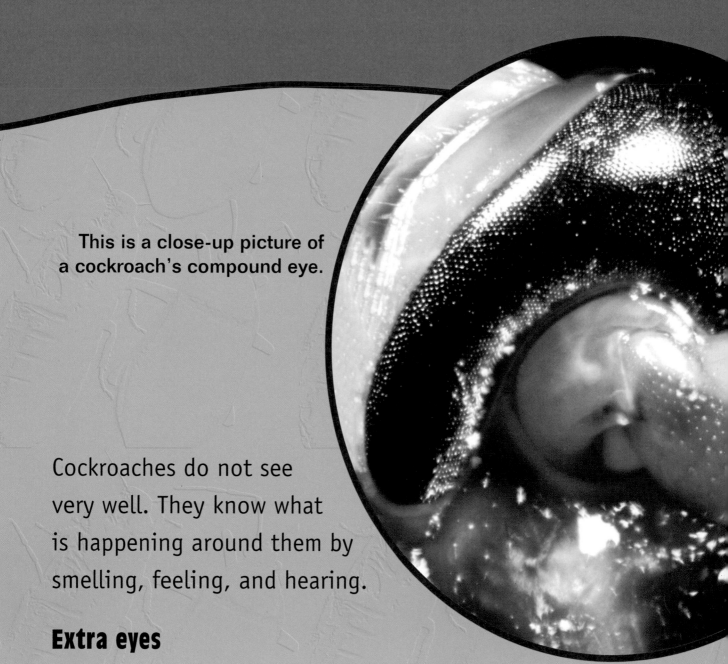

This is a close-up picture of a cockroach's compound eye.

Cockroaches do not see very well. They know what is happening around them by smelling, feeling, and hearing.

Extra eyes

Many cockroaches also have two tiny eyes, one above each compound eye. These eyes probably see only light and dark. Scientists think these eyes may help a cockroach when it is flying.

Antennae and Sensing

A cockroach has two long feelers called **antennae** on its head. The antennae are as long as the cockroach's body.

Sensing with antennae

A cockroach touches and smells things with its antennae. The antennae **sense** the **temperature** around the cockroach. This means it can stay away from places that are too hot or too cold. A cockroach senses movement nearby with its antennae, so it can run away if it needs to.

A cockroach can move its antennae right around itself.

Cleaning antennae

Cockroaches pull their antennae through their mouths so they are cleaned by hairs inside their jaws.

Attracting a mate

A female cockroach makes a smell to attract a male. He smells it with his antennae. When he finds her, they flick each other's antennae for a while. They do this before they **mate.**

More senses

Cockroaches have ears in their knees that can hear very soft sounds. They also have **spines** and hairs on their legs that can feel movements in the air and in the ground.

Cockroaches can taste and smell food with their feet.

15

Legs for Moving

Cockroaches have six legs joined to the **thorax.** Each leg has three main parts, and a long foot. The legs are hairy and covered with **spines.**

How cockroaches move

When a cockroach runs and walks, it moves three legs at a time. The front and back legs on one side step forward at the same time as the middle leg on the other side.

Cockroaches are fast runners. For their size, they can run ten times faster than a person!

Cockroach feet

Each foot has two large
claws on the end.
Cockroaches also have sticky
pads on their feet and front legs. These help
them run fast on smooth, slippery surfaces.

Cockroaches pull themselves up
with their claws when they climb.

17

Wings and Flying

Many cockroaches are strong fliers. They fly to look for food. Flying cockroaches have four wings. **Veins** keep the shape of the cockroach's wings. The veins are hard, hollow tubes.

Cockroaches fold their wings back over their bodies when they are not using them. The back wings are hidden underneath the front wings. The front wings protect the back wings.

Running fast

Brownbanded cockroaches run very fast by spreading their wings and running on their back legs. The air on the wings pushes the end of the body down, making the back legs work better.

Flying

The front wings are thick and the same color as the rest of the cockroach. The cockroach lifts them out of the way while it is flying and flies with its back wings. These wings are very thin and clear.

Flying cockroaches have two wings on each side of the **thorax.**

A cockroach's **thorax** has legs and wings joined to it. There is a **shield** on the back of the thorax.

The **abdomen** has two cerci, like small tail fingers, on the end. If the cerci sense movement, the cockroach's legs start running before it even knows that something is there.

shield

cerci

You can see the shield and cerci in this photograph of the underside of a cockroach.

Many cockroaches have interesting colors and patterns on their shields.

Making sounds

Cockroaches sometimes make squeaking sounds by rubbing the hard edges of the front wings on the back end of the shield.

Some cockroaches make a tapping noise by banging their abdomens on the ground.

Singing cockroaches

Male cinereous cockroaches make singing sounds to attract a female. Both the males and females make a squeaky sound if they are upset. They make the sounds with the wings and the shield on the thorax.

Inside a Cockroach

A cockroach's heart is long and thin. It runs down the middle of the **abdomen.** It pumps clear blood around the body.

How a cockroach gets air

A cockroach's body has ten air holes called **spiracles** on each side. Tiny tubes take air from these holes into the body.

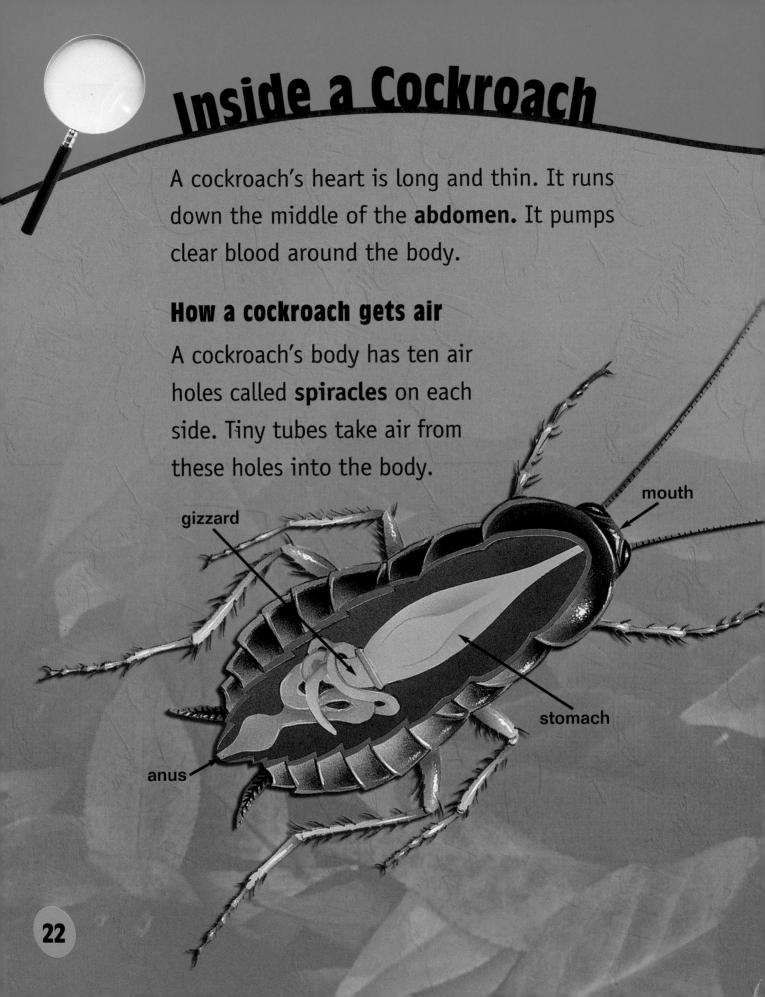

gizzard

mouth

stomach

anus

What happens to food?

A cockroach's food is crushed inside the mouth. It goes down a tube into a large stomach, which is in the first half of the abdomen. The stomach swells up when it is full of food.

Then the food enters a smaller area called a **gizzard.** The gizzard has teeth in it that mash the food up even more. This means a cockroach can eat food with **solid** pieces in it, unlike other insects such as mosquitoes that can only feed on **liquids.**

Waste passes out of the **anus,** on the end of the abdomen.

Cockroach Eggs

Cockroaches grow from eggs. A female **mates** with a male, and then eggs grow inside her. In some cockroaches, the eggs hatch inside the mother. Usually, a mother cockroach lays her eggs first, and then they hatch.

Egg bag

Cockroach eggs are laid in a small egg bag. The bag has a tough skin that protects the eggs. It often has about twenty eggs in it.

Some female cockroaches carry the egg bags with them until the eggs hatch. Others put the bag in a safe place.

abdomen

egg bag

Hatching

The eggs hatch inside the egg bag. The young cockroaches are called **nymphs.** They begin to grow inside the bag. The egg bag has tiny holes in it, so the nymphs can get air. When the nymphs are too big for the bag, it splits open. The cockroach nymphs come out together.

The nymphs come out of the egg bag when they grow too big for it.

Young Cockroaches

When cockroach **nymphs** hatch, they are small, and you can see through their skin. They have no wings, and they have short **antennae.** The **exoskeleton** hardens after one or two hours and becomes colored.

Staying with mother

Nymphs of the Cuban burrowing cockroach stay underneath their mother, or nearby. They do not leave their mother until they have molted twice. By this time they may be up to one month old.

Usually, the nymphs grow up without help from their mother.

This is a newly hatched nymph.

exoskeleton

This young cockroach has left its old exoskeleton.

Growing up

As a young cockroach gets bigger, its hard exoskeleton breaks off to make room for its growing body. This is called molting.

When a growing cockroach has just lost its old exoskeleton, it is soft and white. After a few hours, the cockroach hardens and darkens in color. Then it eats its old exoskeleton. During molting, a cockroach's legs, mouthparts, or antennae might break off accidentally. Then it will grow new ones.

27

Cockroaches and Us

Cockroaches sometimes come into houses, mostly in areas that are warm and wet. Cockroaches like houses because they can find many small places to rest and to lay their eggs.

Cockroaches can be pests because they get into food and leave their droppings behind. Droppings are dirty and may smell. People kill house cockroaches with poisons.

Common pests

The most common pests in houses are the American, Australian, German, Oriental, and brownbanded cockroaches. All of these **species** are found in many parts of the world.

Shy cockroaches

Many people find cockroaches scary, but cockroaches do not bite or sting people. They just run away. They can look scary because they run fast and move suddenly. It is very hard to catch a cockroach because they move away from danger very quickly.

Most cockroaches live in forests and fields. You may not often see them, but they are still there, eating whatever they can or resting in their small homes.

Some people keep cockroaches as pets.

Find Out for Yourself

You may be able to find a place outdoors where there are a lot of leaves, bark, branches, and stones on the ground. You could gently dig into the ground covering with a stick and see if there are any cockroaches underneath.

Books to read

Brimner, Larry Dane. *Cockroaches*. Scholastic Library, 2000.

Claybourne, Anna. *Insects*. Chicago: Raintree, 2002.

Kite, L. Patricia. *Cockroaches*. Minneapolis: Lerner, 2001.

Merrick, Patrick. *Cockroaches*. Eden Prairie, Minn.: Child's World, 2003.

Spilsbury, Louise and Richard Spilsbury. *The Life Cycle of Insects*. Chicago: Heinemann Library, 2003.

Using the Internet

Explore the Internet to find out more about cockroaches. Have an adult help you use a search engine. Type in a keyword such as *cockroaches* or the name of a particular cockroach.

Glossary

abdomen last of the three main sections of an insect

antenna (plural: antennae) feeler on an insect's head

anus hole in the abdomen through which droppings pass

compound made up of smaller parts

exoskeleton hard outside skin of an insect

gizzard stomach for grinding up food

jaw hard mouthpart used for biting and holding food

liquid something that is runny, not hard, such as juice

mate when a male and a female come together to produce young

nocturnal active at night

nymph young stage of an insect; a nymph looks like the adult, only smaller

palp small body part like a finger, near an insect's mouth

predator animal that kills and eats another animal

sense how an animal knows what is going on around it, such as by hearing, seeing, or smelling

shield large, hard, flat object, usually for protection

solid hard, not runny

species type or kind of animal; animals of the same species can produce young together

spine hard, pointed spike

spiracle tiny air hole on an insect's body

temperature measure of hot and cold

thorax chest part of an insect

vein small tube in the body that carries blood; dry veins in insect wings are empty

vibration fast shaking movement

Index

abdomen   8, 9, 20, 21, 22, 23
air holes   22
American cockroaches   28
antennae   8, 11, 14, 15, 26, 27
anus   22, 23
Attaphila fungicola cockroaches   7
Australian cockroaches   28

brownbanded cockroaches   28

cinereous cockroaches   21
claws   17
colors   21
Cuban burrowing cockroaches   26

eggs   24, 25
exoskeleton   5, 9, 26, 27
eyes   8, 12, 13

feet   15, 16, 17
flying   18, 19
food   4, 6, 7, 10, 22, 23, 28

German cockroaches   11, 28
gizzard   22, 23

habitats   6, 7, 28, 29
hairs   9, 15
head   8, 12
heart   22

jaws   11

legs   5, 9, 11, 16, 17, 18, 27

Madeira cockroaches   25
mating   15, 22
molting   26, 27
mouthparts   8, 11, 22, 23, 27

nymphs   23, 26

Oriental cockroaches   28

palps   11
predators   5

senses   11, 14, 15, 17
shield   9, 20, 21
sizes   5
sounds   21
species   5
spines   9, 15, 16
stinking cockroaches   5
stomach   22, 23
swimming   6

thorax   8, 9, 20, 21

wings   9, 18, 19